ABOUT THE AUTHOR

Zozan Yilmaz did her Masters degree in University of Essex's Economics Department where she did a dissertation on Arbitrage Pricing.

She has worked in senior finance positions in various industries from investment banking to central government in London.

Currently she writes on her blog:

www.zozanyilmaz.blogspot.com

...and also works on her new book.

BETWEEN

RECESSION &

DEPRESSION

Zozan Yilmaz

Published 2010 by arima publishing
www.arimapublishing.com

ISBN 978 1 84549 424 7

Printed and bound in the United Kingdom
Typeset in Garamond 11/14

Swirl is an imprint of arima publishing.
arima publishing

ASK House, Northgate Avenue
Bury St Edmunds, Suffolk IP32 6BB
t: (+44) 01284 700321

www.arimapublishing.com

CONTENTS

FOREWORD

We have gone through a painful "credit crunch" Highly indebted economies had to stop and think: "What are we doing?"

Investors thought: "Hold on, we have been investing in products we don't know much about. The control mechanisms - of regulation, collateral-covenants to back loans, credit rating - to avoid defaults are not working."

Governments: "We haven't been regulating enough"

Consumers: "We have been spending more than our income. Ah these credit cards and mortgages, it is their entire fault"

Companies: "We have been running our business with high debt without thinking what if demand for our products declines or stops somehow; do we have any precautionary liquidity?"

Then a big trust crisis explosion. BOOM!!!. The word "Credit" or "Credere" as the Latin origins would call means "to believe". Therefore, a shake of "Credit" multiplied by the world population turned to result with “Economies in trouble”.

Search of scapegoats multiplied. The portfolio included: banks of any sort (central, investment, retail); regulatory bodies; hedge funds; offshore centres; rational expectations theory…

Every single country, industry is affected. “No one was recession proof” Even Olympic Games funded by companies’ sponsorship of $10million-$20million.

Zozan Yilmaz

CHAPTER ONE

THREE DIMENSIONAL INTRODUCTION

Some observations in March 2009 in my blog may be a good starting point:

RECESSION AND NUMBERS

As the recession gets deeper and eyes are on the G20 meeting to be held in April 2009, numbers still manage to surprise with one record after another.

Let's look at some recent unforgettable figures;

On micro basis;
Fedex reported 75 per cent fall in profits on19th March 2009 for its quarter ending on 28th February 2009 from $393 million to $97 million.
AIG reported $60 billion loss for Q4-08, the biggest in US corporate history.
HSBC had £12.5 billion rights issue
Macro basis;

Japan's exports fell by 45.7%, German engineering companies' export orders by 47 per cent in January 2009. 700,000 US job losses were recorded in February 2009.

The changes are very high in percentage and absolute figures when the shortness of the periods is taken into consideration.

The picture gets gloomier when adding the major stock markets' significantly lost values such that; Dow Jones industrial average fell to its lowest level since 1997 with 22 per cent loss since the start of 2009 -as of 2nd March 2009- accompanied by S & P 500's 21 per cent fall.

Q1-09 figures will be very crucial in managing expectations. So far so bad!

CHALLENGE OF COMPARISON

The tools we have today weren't available three decades ago and earlier making it a challenge to compare to either 1929's Great Depression, 1866 or any other.

- There is not much data for the past crashes.
- Sizes of economies are very different in terms of population, GDP etc.
- World powers are different. For example, the power shifted from Britain to United States after the end of

2nd World War. Today, the rank is US, Japan, China, Germany, UK and emerging markets growing significantly.

- Valuation of businesses and economies today can not be explained just by one factor. According to present value of money, the monetary values of 100 years ago and today are very different due to inflation effect. For example, if we assume an average inflation of 3% over the last 100 years in US, then $30million on 1910 will be equivalent of $576million today. As seen in 1866 crisis, Overend, Gurney and Company (OGC) was the greatest discounting house in the world for forty years and could make short term loans to many other bankers. During the 1825 crisis it owed £11million, which is equivalent of £980million in 2008 prices. If we accept this as the value of OGC for the day and compare to value of JP Morgan Chase - today's 4th largest bank in terms of market capitalization - of $94.5billion at depressed values during March 2009, what do we get? How do we explain the difference in values?
- World systems are different. We used to have feudalism between 5th-12th centuries, Mercantilism between 15th-18th century, 19th century version of capitalism etc.
- The monetary systems are different. For example Gold Standard during Great Depression was a barrier

to expand money supply when needed by the economy whereas now central banks are in charge of the macro economy and are able to manoeuvre with money supply.

- Technology is different and in fact the speed it spreads the crisis or optimism is remarkable.
- Globalization is in place where all national economies are closely integrated.
- Global institutions such as IMF, World Bank, G20, are available now since the Second World War. When alarm bells ring, they can act as superman.
- Great Depression's economic effects were tried to be overcome with 2nd World War following protectionist measures whereas today huge fiscal stimulus by all governments around the world are/were applied.

However,

- One tool we can look at is price-earnings ratio (P/E). It will let us assess if stocks are fairly valued in combination with the vision of the economy. Low ratios are typical for recessions and wars, high ratios for economic jumps and bull markets. Before 1929 there were expectations of continuous good news and profit growth, which brought P/E to over 30 for S&P. Reasonable level would be 20-22, 14-15 was the level during the rest of the 20th century. In 1999-2000 it rose over 30.

RECESSION VERSUS DEPRESSION

There are two characteristics of depression:

1. Decline in GDP exceeds 10%
2. It lasts more than three years

Recession on the other hand is defined as two consecutive quarters of negative economic growth.

Wherever we put any crash in terms of category, four characteristics are common:

1. Stock market falls
2. Commercial bankruptcies
3. Bank failures
4. Escalating unemployment

It always starts with optimism feeding bubble and then once confidence evaporates sell off process starts.

What makes a recession a depression is the severity and durability.

One problem we had with credit crunch is the categorization. Negative growth in GDP was longer than two quarters for major economies but didn't last more than three years. So where shall we put it? For example Britain's contraction started in Q4-08 and carried on four quarters until Q3-09.

The depression between 1873 -79 is the longest record in history lasting 65 months.

The more famous Great Depression lasted 43 months between 1929-33 during which GDP of United States fell by 30%.

CHAPTER TWO

HISTORY OF BUBBLES/CRISES/BUSINESS CYCLES

1630s – TULIP MANIA - HOLLAND

Limited information is available about this first speculative bubble.

Before 1633 Holland's tulip trade had been restricted to professional growers and experts, but as the prices rose gradually, many middle-class and poor families started to speculate in the tulip market. It spread to such an extent that estates were mortgaged to buy tulip bulbs for resale at higher prices, rare bulbs were sold at few hundred dollars. But unsustainable price doubt – overnight- brought the crash in 1637. The rest of the story is as usual, wealth shrank at fortune levels.

1720 - MISSISIPI SCHEME - FRANCE

Missisipi was a French company set up in 1684. Businessman John Law acquired a controlling equity in 1717 and the monopoly right to trade with North America from the French government for the next 25 years.

In 1719, the share price of the company went up from 500 livres to 15,000 livres following Law's work. But share price went down to 500 livres again in September 1721 due to decline in confidence. In terms of market capitalization, it fell from 7.5 billion livres to 250 million livres.

The magnitude of the Missisipi Scheme can be understood better if compared to French government's debt of 1.6billion livres and annual expenditures of 150million livres in 1720.

1720 - SOUTH SEA BUBBLE - LONDON

South Sea was a British company set up in 1711, which was promised the monopoly of all trade to Spanish colonies in South America.

The share price of the company bubbled from £128 in January 1720 to £1,050 in June 1720, following false claims of success. In September share price went down to £175.
The magnitude of South Sea bubble can be understood better if compared to British government's debt of £50million in 1719. [£18.3 million of this debt was held by three British corporations; £3.4 million by Bank of England, £3.2 million

by British East India Company, £11.7 million by South Sea Company.]

The other main business cycles by the period are 1825-26, 1837-38, 1846-47, 1866, 1873, 1882, 1893, 1900-1901, 1907. Some are summarized below:

1866 CRISIS

This crisis has similarities to the recent recession.

Firstly it was a banking crisis of discount bank Overend, Gurney and Company (OGC) declaring bankruptcy in May 1866, 66 years after its formation, resulting in inability to provide money for commercial and retail banks in London. London was the financial centre of the world by the time.

Secondly it was the last British Bank people ran on until the Northern Rock in September 2007.

OGC whose core business was buying and selling of bills of exchange at a discount was the greatest discounting house in the world for forty years and could make short term loans to many other bankers. During the 1825 crisis it owed £11million, which is equivalent of £980million in 2008 prices.

The bank made significant long-term investments in railways instead of holding liquid cash reserves. When stock and bond prices – particularly railway stocks – collapsed, commercial credit was tightened rapidly, which resulted in liabilities of £4million and liquid assets of £1million.

OGC asked for a rescue from the Bank of England but it was rejected. Then the panic spread across London, Liverpool, Manchester, Bristol, Norwich and Derby. The financial crisis caused the bank rates to rise to 10% for three months. More than 200 companies, including banks failed as a result.

Gurney's bank was absorbed into Barclays Bank in 1896; Overend and Company was absorbed into National Provincial Bank in 1902

[A reform was put in action where Bank of England got the role of "lender of last resort" for the first time. This prevented the occurrence of the probable crisis in 1890 when Bank of England covered the losses made in investments made in Argentina by the UK bank, Baring.]

1873-79 DEPRESSION

The longest depression in history led to a wave of financial and industrial bankruptcies.

Its has three roots:

1. Rail road industry was the biggest employer after agriculture. Too much capital was invested in rail road projects, which offered late returns.
2. Production of iron and steel stopped. The high demand in both industries was a key driver of the boom in rail road building
3. Investment banks were eagerly financing the capital needed for the growth of the enterprises. However Gold Standard was restricting the monetary policy and the money supply. Therefore money demand was exceeding money supply.

When profit fell below real rate of interest, rail road building stopped, iron and steel production fell steeply. Philadelphia banking and Jay Cooke and Co Investment along with ninety of three-hundred-sixty-four rail road firms went bankrupt. A chain of bank failures followed Jay Cooke.

New York Stock Exchange closed for ten days from September 20 onwards, 18,000 businesses failed between 1873 and 1875, unemployment peaked at 14% by 1876, and wages were cut, and property values fell, corporate profits evaporated.

In Europe, Viennese stock exchange crash followed Viennese bank failures and money lending shrank.

The recovery did not come until 1880 and the rate of growth of international commerce slowed after the two decades following 1873 and did not speed up two decades before World War I.

1893

This was a financial crisis time in United States and Britain. British bank Baring Brothers failed, English pig-iron production fell from 8.3million tonnes in 1889 to 6.7million tonnes in 1892 accompanied by increase in unemployment. In 1893 extensive bank failures arose in United States following a stock market panic.

1900

A recession following a boom represented by 150% increase in US pig-iron production, doubled building permits, 50% increase in cargo traffic, doubled prices and nearly FULL EMPLOYMENT for US economy.

Before the World War I, prosperity and full employment were the main characteristics for Britain. International gold standard as the monetary regime of the day had been unchallenged and working smoothly through the control from London.

1914 CRISIS

The crisis began on 27th July 1914; dollars were sold to buy pounds, raising the $/£ exchange rate to 4.92, which caused gold outflow to Europe. New York Stock Exchange was closed to reduce the sale of American securities and to slow down the demand for gold.

According to Keynes the explanations of the 1914 crisis for Britain were:

1. Inability of foreigners to pay their debts to City firms. This threatened to deprive the Bank of England of the gold it needed to defend the gold standard.
2. Inability of foreigners to pay up on settlement date to the City stockbrokers through whom they had bought shares on the stock exchange.

To protect its reserves, bank rate was increased from 3% on 29 July to 10% on 1 August, and August bank holiday was extended by three days. The stock exchange was closed on 31 July.

The banks' gold reserves were centralised in the Bank of England, the Treasury was empowered to issue emergency currency notes of £1 and 10s. The crisis was over.

AFTER FIRST WORLD WAR

Between April 1919 and April 1920 following Britain's calling off Gold Standard in March 1919 and sterling's fall against the dollar from $4.70 to $3.40 between April 1919 and February 1920:

- Interest rates were low at 4%
- Monthly inflation was 4% encouraging borrowing. Because differential between inflation and borrowing was creating opportunities for arbitrage profit.
- Heat of the economy was high with daily floating, sale and purchase of companies.

In order to cool down the economy; bank rate was put up to 7% from 4% on 15 April and held at this level for a year following new taxes imposed by the government. The result was:

- First consumer then investment spending fell, followed by prices

- Unemployment rose to 22%
- Output fell by 15% for the next twelve months
- Money wages fell by one-third
- Wholesale prices fell by half.
- USD/GBP exchange rate fell from 4.70 to 3.40

Economy was under full employment between two world wars driven by too low profit expectations and deflation.

On 7th July 1923 unemployment was 11.4% at 1.3million. Bank/base rate was raised from 3% to 4% to correct the fall in sterling against the dollar from 4.70 in March to 4.56 in June.

GREAT DEPRESSION

Great depression's severity of functioning as a benchmark for "depression" guided us since 2008.
29th of October was the crash day for stock market naming 28th and 29th of October as Black Monday and Black Tuesday respectively.
Unemployment was 25% in US, 20% in UK,
Price-earning ratios bottomed at below 10,
Nearly half of the banks in US failed.
The characteristics of the preceding boom period were:

Ratio of "time deposits" to "demand deposits" rose from 28.6% to 44.7% between 1919 and 1928. This is considered as a vital liquid reserve by the industry and signals that money was being saved rather than invested and this was a barrier to full employment of resources.

Amazing borrowing between 1925 and 1928 fuelled rapid economic growth, and stock market boom.

Interest rates rose gradually from early 1928 onwards shooting the US economy's slowdown

After the pre-shock:

Federal Reserve lowered the interest rate from 6% to 2.5%, and applied deficit creating expansionary fiscal policy within a year.

Government started wage maintenance agreements to prevent falling wages and therefore consumption element of GDP.

In April 1931, sterling crisis occurred following City's borrowing short and lending long with a result of £254million of short-term debtor position. The situation got so serious that City's and government's solvency was questioned.
In mid 1931 a new economic decline developed, which resulted in a new depth in 1932-3. Stock market more than

halved. Federal Reserve responded to this by tightening credit. The stock markets declined, rush for liquidity brought bank failures.

Overvalued exchange rates, deflationary constraints, weak economy and unemployment brought cancellation of Gold Standard by Britain in September 1931.

Bank rate was kept at 2% between June 1932 and 1939.

March 1933 was the worst point of Depression with bank failures, panic, closure of banks, GDP down by 30%, industrial production down by 45%, unemployment up to 25% from 3% in 1929. Nearly 13million Americans were unemployed.

Other countries in the order of % GDP decline were Germany's GDP by 20%, France's by 16%, UK's 6%.

The spreaders of depression to such severe levels were gold standard, declining trade, protectionist policies and weak business confidence.

From mid 1933, a slow recovery started, unemployment started to fall below 20%. US's GDP started to increase by an average of 9% between 1933 and 1937. Wall Street prices trebled by 1936.

Economic stability and instability has turned into a major concern for economists after Great Depression.

In 1933 the banking law of Glass-Stegall was enacted, which separated different activities of banking; mainly commercial banking from investment banking.

SOME OTHER 20TH CENTURY CRISES

Between 1950 and 1973 GDP per capita increased by 4.5% per year on average. Countrywide for example Japan grew by 7.3% per year on average. US, UK and Canada's growth was low. Governments were active in economy. For Western Europe, governments made one-forth to one-third of GDP. Literacy was high as well in Europe.

1970S CRISIS:

This is characterized by severe recession at the top of inflation.

The drivers were various, but mainly:

- Abandonment of fixed exchange rates
- Liberalization of financial systems
- Low taxes

- Shooting oil prices

The first three drove the asset-price boom.

1987 STOCK MARKET CRASH

The main cause was the tighter monetary policy. But the pain remained limited because of the shortness of duration with six to eight months.

Gordon Gemmill's article titled "Did Option Traders Anticipate the Crash? Evidence from the Volatility Smiles in the UK with US Comparisons" informs that there was no volatility prior to crash standing at 19.1% on 15th October 1987, peaking at 96.7% on 22nd October and falling back to 36.4% on 1st December. Pre-crash volatility was 18.3 whereas post-crash was 19.8%.

John Calverley's "Bubbles and How to Survive Them" stated:

- In two days share prices fell over 30% in the US, and UK.
- Most other countries, cut interest rates in the following days and weeks.
- This helped the markets to regain their October peaks within a year or so. It also gave investors some

comfort that the central banks, at least to a degree, were on their side. This was sometimes referred to as the "Greenspan put", because it seemed to offer downside protection to investors in rather the same was as a put option.

In 1987, Alan Greenspan took Fed chairman position and his interest reduction policy started from 1989 onwards.

JAPAN'S 1980s BUBBLE AND BUST

After Japan removed its strict banking regulation, the extra credit fuelled asset prices. The main assets affected were stock and property. When the bust came, land prices fell more than 90% while stock prices fell 80%.

SWEDEN'S BANKING CRISIS IN THE 1990S

Sweden liberalized its banking system in 1985 by removing the limits on interest rates and credit and extending lending of banks for commercial property. Boom started and carried on until the second quarter of 1990.

During the bust between 1990 and 1993, economy contracted by 6.1%, fiscal deficit was 12% of GDP. In 1993, it started to grow slowly, it was 1994 summer when healthy banks and strong growth were realised.

ASIA 1997/8

The crisis was shouted with the currency collapse of Thai Baht. Thailand, Indonesia, South Korea were the most deeply affected countries. Capital outflows were the main driver of currency collapses.

Massive rise and successive fall of property and stock prices, IMF bailout of $40billion were seen.

US 2001

Inflation dropped sharply in 2002 and by 2003 was below 1% and still falling, making deflation a concern. Price-earnings ratios were 15 compared to 10 during 1930s and 1970s.

INSTITUTIONS SET UP AS RESPONSE TO CRASHES OR CHANGING DYNAMICS

- *Securities and Exchange Commission* in response to 1929 crash to regulate brokerages and other tasks such as margin lending (which is the fact that stockbrokers borrow to buy stocks) – Today hedge funds do this to a large extent (termed leverage). Investment trusts is another example. The more it spreads the riskier the system gets.

- *International Monetary Fund (IMF)* is the global body set up after the World War II to promote world trade, investment and economic growth by maintaining convertible currencies at stable exchange rates. Countries with balance of payments deficits would borrow and therefore solve their domestic problems with their own resources rather than spreading to other countries through policies like devaluation, deflation, exchange controls. Advising borrowing governments, stabilizing currency exchange rates and financing balance of payments deficits have been the three main functions.
- *World Bank* is the global bank set up after World War II along with IMF. Its first loans were for reconstruction of Western Europe. From 1950s onwards its focus moved to developing countries' infrastructure projects such as building roads, hydroelectric damns, airports.
- *G8* set up in 1975 as a response to 1973's oil crisis.
- *G20* set up in 1999 reflecting the fact that developing economies are gaining power.

- *Financial Services Enquiries Commission* set up in 2009 to investigate the causes of the credit crunch.

THE FINANCIAL CRISIS INQUIRY COMMISSION

We are seeing United States initiative for investigations regarding the causes of the recent crisis. We have been discussing, reading about these since 2007 but the commission has put them in a more organized structure under 22 headings ranged from credit rating agencies, global imbalances, corporate governance, derivatives to securitisation.

On the positive side:

1. US determination to lead the exit is persistent
2. . A rich mix will be available in hearings from head of top investment banks to regulators and independent experts.

On the question mark side:
Will it cause high public expectations or indifference?

CHAPTER THREE

REVIEW OF 19TH & 20TH CENTURIES

Two centuries are quite different and useful to review.

- 19th century is characterized by full employment, low population. 20th century is a massive increase in population and highly likely to be a factor in frequency of crises. World resources are not enough. [21st century population already above 6billion and expected to increase one third by 2050.]

  Europe's population started to increase from 1740 onwards after the stagnation between mid seventeenth – mid eighteenth centuries. It had risen to 200million by 1800; 400million by 1900 when total world population was 900 million and 1.6billion respectively. Global population continued to increase but Europe was not proportionate; by 1950 standing at 550million of 2.5billion world population.

- Gold standard created both stable exchange and price level in the 19th century combined with special conditions at the time such as absence of large fluctuations in value of gold due to large gold discoveries going parallel with business needs. It also prevented politicians from printing money easily.

- The volume of global foreign trade per capita in 1913 was 25 times larger than the level in 1800. Europe made up 60% of imports and exports during 19th century.

Exponential growth in international trade from 1840 onwards was the main driver of growth. Adam Smith and David Ricardo's Wealth of Nations and Comparative Advantage Theory respectively formed the theoretical basis.

Three themes of Adam Smith's Wealth of Nations are:

1. Object of political economy is growth of national wealth,
2. Division of labour is the major cause of productivity. David Ricardo's Comparative Advantage Theory took this further, which provided strong arguments in favour of free trade and specialisation of labour.
3. Wealth is composed of commodities, is a flow concept similar to today's GDP and is outcome of productive processes not precious metals.

Therefore, what makes a society wealthier is more complex social division of labour. The famous 'increasing returns to scale' is explained by division of labour; meaning people can specialise in the production of a single commodity and then increase their productivity.

As a defender of free trade the argument was that: Government should stay out of economic life, and just keep law and order.

- The world economy was at very high level of integration and interdependence at the beginning of the 20th century.

- In the first quarter of 20th century, there was a lack in discovery of new gold deposits.

- At micro level, 20th century was joint-stock companies, which are run by salaried managers controlled by shareholders.

- Early 1970s witnessed economic and political changes such as abandoned fixed exchange rates, liberalized financial systems, less effective trade unions, cut taxes. All escorted asset-price booms of the 1980s and 1990s.

- Profits were low in 1970s with effect of high oil prices. But from 1980s onwards the trend was recovered profits, spread of share options and incentives, and rise in commodity prices with opening of Russian, Indian, Chinese economies.

- Wealth accumulated remarkably. Forbes 400 richest peoples' wealth multiplied from $92bn in 1982 to $1.25trillion in 2006.

WHY DID THE FREQUENCY OF CRISES INCREASE SO MUCH?

John Calverley provides answer to this question in "Bubbles and how to survive them" as below:

1) Widespread asset ownership: 50 years ago only a small proportion of the population was holding assets in small-scale deposits whereas today more than 75% of the developed countries' population own assets in the form of stocks, mutual funds, houses or pensions.
2) Easiness of asset trading: Internet made immediate transparent prices available on electronic quotation systems, which was a facility only big financial institutions had access to in the past.
3) New asset backed economy brings volatility.

We need to note that not only did the frequency of crises increase in 20th century but also they spreaded to a much wider geographical region.

HOW WAS IT BEFORE?

During feudalism between the 5th and 12th centuries, nineteenth-century capitalism; economic wealth and power were concentrated in the hands of few land-owners, small group of capitalists or an elite group of bureaucrats.

SOME BACKGROUND ON THE PREVIOUS FORMS:

- FEUDALISM

The simplest way to look at feudalism is as non-existence of public authority & non-centralized governments. Local lords implemented admin and legal functions. Its rise in 5th century is to do with disappearance of Western half of Roman Empire (eastern half continued as Byzantine Empire) and its fall in 12th century is to do with appearance of kingdoms as operational government units.

- NINETEENTH - CENTURY CAPITALISM

Nineteenth-century is the end of Mercantilism, which is the first form of capitalism.

MERCANTILISM

Mercantilism started with the discovery of America in 1492 and lasted until end of 18th century according to which positive balance of trade is the only source of wealth. During the initial stage of bullionism, focus is on buying cheap and selling expensive whereas in the second stage , it shifts to foreign trade, and competitiveness. 18th century England's capitalism moved from commerce to industry.

European states quickly established colonies, took advantage of large flow of gold and silver from Peru and Mexico. International trade became incredibly important; significance of merchants increased both in international and domestic economies. Use of money became widespread. Strong national states arose.

During 18th century; building societies were invented and carried over to today. Chelsea Building Society, which is UK's fifth-largest today was founded in 1875. It was one of the hardest hit by current recession's down-grades from A2 to Baa3.

19th century is a very intensive period in terms of number of developments happening. We can see the impact of capitalist economy in terms of higher benefit. Joseph Schumpeter's diagnosis was that capitalist economy is quicker to seize sudden opportunities and thus higher productivity due to capitalist culture baked with capable entrepreneurs and expert bankers.

- The old empires of Spanish, Portuguese, Chinese, Holy Roman, Mughal were replaced by United States, and British - German empires.
- After Napoleonic wars between 1803-15 – following the French Revolution in 1789, British Empire became the dominant power of the world.
- The Industrial Revolution began in Europe.
- Europe's population grew exponentially during the century from 200million to 400million.
- Britain abolished slavery in 1834.
- Gold Standard was first put in place in Britain in 1821.

Under the light of these changes; 19th century was a period of political liberalism with free trade, balanced budgets, gold standard.

CHAPTER FOUR

BANKING & ITS EVALUATION AFTER WORLD WAR II

Half a century ago banks extended loans with basic calculations when deciding whether to lend or not.

From 1970s onwards, the world turned into a risk abundant planet due to reasons mentioned in Chapter Two of this book. The response of the industry to this new trend was:

1) Selling their credit risk through credit derivatives on to third-party investors in the blossoming capital markets

2) Adopting complex computer-based systems for measuring credit risk

Value at risk (VAR) was the standard credit and market risk measure. 1987's crash was the driver of the concept and first started to be used by the industry from mid 1990s, initially by JP Morgan. It mainly tries to estimate the extreme losses and reasons the undefined losses being due to factors such as illiquid or closed markets. Very roughly it tells the maximum possible loss with x% of confidence (confidence is usually 95%), which was applied from statistics' "confidence interval" concept.

It was blamed to incentivise taking excess risks and playing a big role in recent financial crisis.

COLLATERALISED DEBT OBLIGATONS (CDO)

These are asset-backed securities and were developed when bankers created mortgage-linked bonds often mixed with other credit derivatives. In 2006 and 2007 $450bn of CDO securities were produced, which were not being traded but sold to banks' off-balance sheet entities such as Structured Investment Vehicle (SIVs) or left in books. Most banks had no market price for those CDOs, but valued them by theoretical calculations from models.

EXCHANGE TRADED FUNDS (ETFS)

First created in 1993, ETFs typically track stock market indices or asset class. Investors can buy and sell ETFs on stock exchange during the day. Value of US ETFs peaked in 2007 before falling to $495bn in Jan 2009. As observed by Economist, the value of the market has grown to $1trillion globally as of end of 2009. "The industry has been growing faster than hedge funds, but with much less negative publicity".

ETFs are the new shining star of the financial markets.

DERIVATIVES IN GENERAL CREDIT DEFAULT SWAPS IN PARTICULAR

Derivatives, which are made of futures, options, and swaps, have been the instruments for managing, controlling and hedging risk against fall in prices over the past three decades. They are a response to the increasing volatility in financial markets – interest rates, exchange rates, and asset prices - , reduction in foreign exchange controls. However, they are risky.

Futures and exchange-traded options are regulated markets, which are highly standardized, limited to few goods and they have a few expirations per year. They are traded on exchanges such as Chicago Board of Trade, London International Financial Futures and Options Exchange, Tokyo International Financial Futures Exchange. They are made of contracts between each original counterparty and the exchange or clearing house

Swap market has emerged due to their flexible nature in contrast to limitations of futures and exchange-traded options markets. They are customized in accordance to the needs of the counterparties. For example counterparties can select the $ amount they want to swap, the exact maturity they need. They are unregulated. These made them very popular across all industries. Even non- financial companies made up $50trillion of outstanding contracts in the interest-rate and foreign exchange markets recently.

Derivatives were blamed in February 1995's collapse of Barings PLC – London based merchant bank - following $1billion of losses made on futures contracts trade in Asian markets by a trader in Singapore. In 1980s London's Hammersmith and Fulham Council made huge losses in derivatives contracts when interest rates moved against it. Procter & Gamble had made huge losses in 1994 as well. In 1994, securities regulators from 16 countries discussed and agreed on measures to strengthen supervision of futures exchanges and any problems could be dealt locally to prevent an international domino effect.

Credit default swaps (CDS) sold by banks, hedge funds and others are functioning as a kind of insurance to cover the losses on certain securities for the case of default. Municipal bonds, corporate debt and mortgage securities are the securities that CDS apply for. The buyer pays a premium for this insurance over a period of time. Trading volume of CDSs is the main problem in the sense that an average CDS can be traded / swapped from one investor to another 15 or 20 times. So when default happens, the insured party doesn't know who is responsible for compensating the default. Insurers had to write-down on their CDS holdings.

As a solution; central clearing houses were suggested to provide information on the involved parties of the transactions

The growth in figures is amazing.

As stated in Gillian Tett's book of Fool's Gold; in 1987, International Swaps and Derivatives Association calculated the total volume of derivatives contract as $865billion.

"Between 1992 and 1993 the value of the deals rose from $5.3 trillion to $8.5trillion.

Deals were becoming more complex, and were being sold to a wider range of customers. The original customers for swaps had been large international corporations or banks, with sophisticated treasury departments and investment analysts – Coca-Cola, IBM, and the World Bank. By 1992, small banks, mid-sized companies, pension funds and many other asset managers were joining the market. And more and more of them were turning to derivatives not to control future risks, but to make big gambles and realize big returns. "

By the start of 2000 Bank for International Settlements (BIS) predicted the value of the Over The Counter (OTC) derivatives deals at $100trillion. By late 2008 the same value stood at $600trillion.

(CDS) costs also rose for Eastern European countries' debt due to concern over their economies. For example cost of insuring Hungary's debt rose to 580 basis points, which means €580,000 cost to insure €10million debt.

RISK MANAGEMENT

Markowitz 1959 model on portfolio selection forms the basis of risk-management. This model provides the criteria of choosing among assets for risk-averse investors. Basically he says that if return on assets has a normal distribution, or if the utility function is quadratic, rational investors maximise their expected utility by choosing the assets that provide the best combination of mean-variance of returns (i.e. they choose efficient portfolios)

This forms the basis of "Efficient Market Hypothesis", which means:

- Market prices include all acknowledged information and therefore derivatives could be priced precisely. Also correlations between stocks would act as hedge when you buy two stocks moving in opposite directions.

- Sample of returns have a normal distribution; which would accept occurrence of extreme events such as crashes but "RARELY".

- We can measure the trade-off between risk and return. The higher the risk the higher the return and therefore equities is the best performing asset class.

This is a major concept, which was blamed to be failed recently. With regards to first proposition; As Jeremy Siegel's book "Stocks for the Long Run" indicates; correlations change in crash times.

There are three forms of efficient markets:

- **Weak form efficiency:** Future price movements can not be predicted by analyzing the price from the past.
- **Semi-strong form efficiency:** Prices adjust to publicly available information quickly.

- **Strong form efficiency:** Prices reflect all information, public and private and it is not possible to beat the market.

US and UK are counted as examples of "semi-efficient markets".

RISK ATTITUDES

Finance theory categorises investors' attitudes to risk under three headings as risk averse, risk neutral and risk lover. The first is where investor prefers less risk to more, second where investor is indifferent to risk and finally the third where investors prefer more risk for less.

Conventional wisdom is that investors are risk averse. The higher the risk they associate with a particular investment, the higher the return they will demand. According to portfolio theory, the main risk investors will ask return for is the systematic/market risk, which is the part that can not be removed through diversification and measured by beta. – The correlation of any stock's return with the market-

During the last three decades of boom period, we breached this wisdom by taking risks beyond the capacity funded by debt assuming the bull market will go on. The result is well known as a global financial system brought to the edge of collapse.

Now we are all risk averse. UK government's failed bond auction on 25th March is the evidence of how dramatically risk averse we have been. Germany had the same painful experience earlier this year. We are used to experience this with emerging markets but when it is the world's 5th and 4th largest economies respectively you are talking about, then you stop and think.

The investors' concern is understandable when you look at the facts that planned UK government borrowing of £350 billion for financial years of 2009-10 & 2010-11 is GREATER than total borrowed by successive rulings and governments of Britain between 1691 and 1997. Mervyn King's loud concern makes more sense after taking this fact into consideration.

The yield on the 10-year UK Gilt climbed 7bp to 3.02 per cent in the third week of March 2009. A sign that investors are nervous about buying UK government debt and asking for premium for the perceived risk

Is there another option? Domestic demand is contracting mainly by consumption and investment items of GDP. Government item needs to increase its share to fill the big hole left from the former two and borrowing is the only funding option.

Monetary policy is already in place with bank rates near zero. Four million tracker mortgages will enjoy reduction in the mortgages they pay, if not yet so and hopefully this will boost consumption. Low interest rates should theoretically cause investment to increase but the current climate is making this item most difficult to play its role given the reluctance of the banks to lend, uncertainty surrounding the global economy, spare capacity. Another barrier for private investment item is the crowding effect created by the government borrowing.

But there is no solution to keep all sides happy. One or more sides have to pay for the cost. In this instance it seems to be partly private investment in lack of fund, depressed demand and government in having to bailout the private sector.

Let's hope these efforts give fruits soon.

CHAPTER FIVE

AN OVERVIEW OF THE CREDIT CRUNCH: THE FIRST DEEP CRASH OF THE 21ST CENTURY

A. MACRO

1. UNEMPLOYMENT

During 1861-1957's UK, relationship between rate of change in money wages and unemployment was being explained by Phillips Curve originated by the economist A. William Phillips. Phillips found that changes in wages could be explained by unemployment for the average of the period except the exceptional circumstances such as rise in import prices. Low wage occurs because of high unemployment vice versa. Phillips curve suggested that low unemployment and low inflation are not complements.

But as of the beginning of 21st century, low unemployment could persist with relatively low wages, contradicting Phillips curve.

Independent of what happens with wages; in US; unemployment number increased from 7.5million to 15million between December 2007 and December 2009, doubling in two years from a cumulative figure. 2008 was declared as the year of biggest payroll losses. Relative figure in particular continued to rise, from 7% in December 2008 to hitting over 10% at the end of 2009.

Similarly in UK the number increased from 2million to 2.5million between the same periods. The reasons for the lower increase in absolute numbers are:

- One year time lag between the start of the crisis for the two sides of the Atlantic.
- US has a population of 300million whereas UK has 60million. Most updated working population in US is around 158million whereas it is around 31million in UK.

Some other macro global changes are:

US incremental unemployment was 500thousand in December 2008 with a jump to 6.3% from 5.9% in December 2007. For the same period; the jump for Canada is to 6.7% from 4.7%; UK to 6% from 5.3%; France to 7.9% from 7.8%; Spain to 13.4% from 8.6% ; Italy to 6.7% from 6.4%; South

Korea to 3.1% from 3%; Japan to 3.9% from 3.8%, Sweden to 6.2% from 6.1%.

Two economies, which recorded fall in unemployment for the same period, are Brazil and Germany with Brazil's falling to 7.6% from 8.2% and Germany's falling to 7.1% from 8%.

Q1-09 & UNEMPLOYMENT

First quarter's draft figures started to be appearing. US March unemployment was announced to be 746,000 and February, January were updated upwards to 706,000, 655,000 respectively (Note1). This reminded me of Fibonacci numbers where the next number is bigger than the previous in a series of numbers such that :

0 - 1 - 1 - 2 - 3 - 5 - 8 - 13 - 21 - 34 - 55 - 89 - 144 - 233 - 377 - 610 - 987 - 1597 - 2584 – 4181

The only difference with monthly US unemployment figures is the lack of existence of a relationship between the numbers. With Fibonacci numbers any number starting from the third is the sum of the previous two as can be seen below:

0+1=1

1+1=2

2+3=5

3+5=8 etc

US unemployment figures has been on an upward slope, thankfully not as bad as Fibonacci numbers would state - it would have been 1,361,000 in March as total of January and February!- although it is not still going down!

If we make the picture even bigger; of the 112 million US employees in payroll – as of 2002 statistics - 56.4 million are in small businesses AND many small businesses are expected to close in the near future. Depressed demand and dried lending is making life difficult mostly for them. They are least likely to get government bailout.

On global scale; UK unemployment is expected to increase from two million cumulative number to three million by 2011, global unemployment to increase by fifty-one million in 2009 in the worst case scenario.

We were talking to an entrepreneur friend of mine the other day and one possibility we were both concerned was war. Unemployment is the strongest indicator of this probability. OECD is already talking about having double digit percentage of unemployment at the end of 2009.

Watching the protests against the G20 meeting held in London, one protester dying, many being injured, taken under custody remind the history of wars.

Is there a sun shining somewhere? May be the determination shown by G20 leaders to fight, lending $1.1trillion to IMF and opening the channels for IMF to lend from the markets if necessary. Markets welcomed this determination with Nasdaq, Dow Jones, Nikkei all up.

We hope to get there eventually without having a Third World War. Fingers crossed!

Note1: Figures were updated on Friday, the 3rd April as Jan: 741,000; Feb: 651,000; Mar: 663,000

OPTIMISM IS IN THE AIR

According to Financial Times, increase in US unemployment is 11thousand in November. An incredible improvement from six digits to five digits in one single month.

When we look at the monthly trend during 2009 with the chart as below, November can be the end of the increase from 7.5million in December 2007 to 15million today.

US is leading the world out of this recession. 11thousand is almost 0 when considering the October figure of 195thousand. Numbers speak louder than words.

2. CREDIT

Dick Fuld's, the former head of Lehman Brothers, observation in 2007 that "whereas credit grows arithmetically, it shrinks geometrically" is a good starting point to look at the credit issue.

Some very big picture figures to help us visualise the debt trap we have are: US household debt of 129% of disposable income and UK's personal debt levels of £1.46trillion as of December 2009.

Auto, private equity, mortgage, hedge funds are some of the industries at the extremes.

Private equity is an industry where investors commit to tie up their capital for several years. EMI in music industry and Boots are some examples of private equity owned giants in UK. Globally the industry has $400billion of debt, which needs to be paid back in the next 4-5 years.

Hedge funds shrunk by more than 40% as of beginning of September 2009 covering the previous 18 months according to Hedge Fund Intelligence

The source of the shrink is the drying funding in money markets.

There is some cooling down signs such as: Bank lending in US has fallen from $7.14trillion in May 2009 to $6.78trillion in September 2009. Credit card spending fell by $1.25 trillion as of mid October 2009. Global volume of loan markets dropped to $411.8billion in Q1-09, which is a 53% fall compared to last year and the fall has been during the last seven quarters consecutively.

Keynes's central proposition was that there is no automatic mechanism in a credit money economy to keep savings and investment equal. The reason is to do with the fact that banks create money.

The only short-run balancer a credit economy has is banking policy. Under the gold standard the Bank of England was prevented from setting bank rate low enough to allow a level of investment equal to what community wanted to save, which resulted in mass unemployment whereas today central banks can create money. All recent quantitative easing policies of buying government bonds to pump money into the economy saved the world from falling the cliff.

GOLD STANDARD SYSTEM

It is the monetary system in which gold is used as a medium of international payments, exchange rates between countries is fixed. It first started in Britain in 1821. Full gold standard that existed from 1870s to 1914 let the gold to be sold in unlimited quantities at a fixed price in convertible paper money per unit weight of the metal.

By 1928, gold standard had been practically re-established but because of the relative scarcity of gold, most nations adopted a gold-exchange standard, in which they supplemented their central-bank gold reserves with currencies (US$ and £) that were convertible into gold at a stable rate of exchange. The gold-exchange standard collapsed during the Great Depression of the 1930s, and by 1937 not a single country remained on the full gold standard.

Advantages of gold standard are:

- It limits the governments/banks' power in creating inflation through issuing excess paper currency.
- It creates certainty in international trade through fixed pattern of exchange rates.

Disadvantages are:

- It may be a barrier in the flexibility of the supply of money because the supply of gold is not close the growing needs of the world economy's money supply needs.
- It is not possible for a country to isolate its economy from depression or inflation in the rest of the world.
- The process of adjustment for a country with a payments deficit can be long and painful whenever an increase in unemployment or a decline in the rate of economic expansion occurs.

SEMI GOLD STANDARD BACK WITH BRETTON WOODS

Bretton Woods Agreement started after the Second World War. Many countries fixed their exchange rates to US dollar following US's promise to fix the gold price at $35 per ounce so that each currency pegged to the US$ had a fixed value in terms of gold.

In 1958 a version of gold standard was re-established such that main European countries offered free convertibility of their currencies into gold and dollars for international payments.

The system broke down in 1971.

3. CREDIT RATING

Three major credit rating agencies of S&P, Moodys. Fitch have been a main guide for investors in assessing companies' creditworthiness. They have been rating companies based on computer models and the risk of future default was assessed using past data. Domino effect was measured based on the correlation between products.

Relevant blog posts are as below:

CREDIT RATING AGENCIES

Should credit rating agencies function as informative organizations after things happen or as a forewarning mechanism?

When S&P downgraded five state-backed companies in Dubai after $59billion of delayed payments, presumably it is targeting to help for avoidance of future casualties.

They have been one of the most criticized bodies during this recession and any potential default risk just brings them back under the scrutiny of the public.

S&P's, Moody's, Fitch will be under more pressure to meet the dynamic nature of the current economy and update their ratings more often.

S&P's responded to that pressure by downgrading 20 European companies yesterday, highlighting the default risk until 2011.

Some other examples are:

Macro: S&P's downgrading of Spain from triple-A credit rating in mid-January 2009 following weakening public finances; Japan again from triple-A credit rating in 2001.
Micro: S&P's downgrading of G.M. in the first week of October 2008. Moody's downgrading of nine largest UK building societies in mid-April 2009 of which total assets range between £4.3billion (Norwich and Peterborough) to £179billion (Nationwide).

BRITAIN'S CREDIBILITY

Alistair Darling's budget figures dominated the agenda of the week. There is pretty much agreement that he is too optimistic in growth forecasts of 2009, 2010 and 2011 with 3.5 per cent contraction, 1.25 per cent expansion, and 3.5 per cent expansion respectively. IMF forecasts contraction for both 2009 and 2010, which I also believe is the case.

With current government spending plans, Britain needs £175bn in 2009 and another £173bn in 2010. Alistair Darling is contradicting his 2010 growth forecast with the most fundamental fact that he needs pretty much the same amount of government spending in 2010 unless the government spending causes an increase in household consumption and/or business investment. Considering the extent of unemployment, consumption is not the right candidate. Can the doubled capital allowance or £750m technology investment fund fill the gap through increased investment spending? We can't tell under current uncertainty.

The tricky bit is the funding of the government spending. Gilts will be the major mechanism, and you have to be CREDIBLE to be able to attract investors. Now, Alistair Darling's figures don't add up and there is a huge competition to sell government bonds from USA, European countries, Japan. US is planning to issue $2,000bn in the fiscal year from last October onwards, Euro zone governments $1,035bn for this financial year, Japan $449bn, and UK $262bn. Needless to mention the multinational companies selling corporate bonds to the same market segment.

Investors have a huge choice and little confidence! They are showing this through higher yields on gilts and higher basis point on credit default swaps. Former being the investors' premium for higher risk and latter being cost of insuring against default on UK gilt.

If both yields and basis points keep on upward slope, then UK's AAA credit rating may come under threat, may not be able to raise the target funds from gilt sales and it may be likely to knock IMF's door for bailout funds as in 1976. Ratings Agency Moody's confirmed on Friday, the 24th April that it is not considering UK government's credit rating for a possible downgrade. Let's hope Moody's doesn't change his mind for the next two years.

GREECE'S CREDIBILITY

Greece has been giving alarm bells for a while that its credit default swap spread jumped from 15bp two years ago to 208bp during the last week of November and 225bp few days ago.

And Greece's credit rating was downgraded by Fitch from A- to BBB+.

Financing a debt of €10million will cost €225thousand to insure against default. Nearly half of what it costs to some Eastern European countries.

Contagion effect already started to cause other EU economies being effected as well. Spain already warned by S&P, - badly hit by the housing market - has potential to be the next casualty.

US CREDIT RATING

Moodys's warning last week over US's credit rating that triple A might be under pressure if growth was not robust is risking all relieves. Is the timing right when exit from expansionary policies and worries of what will happen with the bubble inside the bubble are the main concerns.

May be time to ask: "Do we need reverse-refunds of triple A until the economy is back to normal"?

4. GDP

With the crash two effects were seen on GDP:

- The split changed.
- Growths fell

Consumption is forming the biggest part of US GDP with a split of 70%. UK is similar with nearly two-third of GDP.

With US, December 2008 was the sixth consecutive month that US consumers lowered spending by 1% followed by 0.8% in November. It has fallen by 3% for UK in 2009, which was the biggest decline in the past 60 years.
Governments covered many market functions during the time the markets signed off-sick. US Treasury's "stress tests" of banks, UK's bank rescues are some of them.
Barclays Capital estimated that Federal Reserve's balance sheet would reach 29% of GDP by the end of 2009 from 7% in 2008.

In terms of overall GDP growth/contraction on annualized terms; the last quarter of 2008 was a contraction for most of the economies. US's fell by 6.2%; UK's by 6%, Sweden's by 9.3%; Canada's by 3.4%; Denmark's by 3.9% etc. Japan's 2008 GDP growth was 0.7% down from 2.1% in 2007.

For China the story was different, they kept growing like India and Indonesia during the recession but just the speed slowed down. First quarter of 2009 witnessed an annualised growth of 6.1%, which is the lowest growth since 1992 when quarterly GDP data started to be published. Chinese banks responded to that by issuing new loans worth $670billion for the period.
In terms of sectors; US manufacturing activity contracted at its sharpest pace for nearly 30 years in December 2008.

It was a milestone to see France, Japan, Germany and US growing again in 2009. Here is what I have written in my blog:

THE BIG ANNOUNCEMENT - I

FED's Chairman Ben Bernanke made the long awaited announcement on the 16th of September that recession is over for USA.
I have been waiting to hear this for a long time, more impatiently after Germany, France and Japan declared growth for quarter two - 0.3%, 0.3%, and 0.6% respectively. - The fact that Bernanke made the announcement before quarter-three ended is signalling that I am not the only one. The main reasoning is the expectation that USA should lead the world out of this Great Recession earlier than anyone else as it led into it the first. Basically FIFO – First in First Out - principle

of inventory management was my presumption but we had LIFO – Last in First Out – this time.

I am not convinced yet though, will need to see at least quarter-three & four figures in growth before making the judgement that it is really heading to be over. Forecasts lost their credibility with daily-weekly-monthly changing announcements during the first half of 2009.

On the positive side US monthly unemployment figures have fallen from an approximate average of 700k per month in first quarter to 539k in April, 345k in May, and finally 216k in August. Downward slope is a good sign. Also improving consumer confidence reflected through increased sales is supportive.

On the negative side though, there is still a nervously waiting banking sector, focused on saving its own life – through increasing high quality Tier-1 capital- and can barely help anyone else. The sector is still in intensive care except few big names on Investment Banking side such as Goldman Sachs and JP Morgan Chase. Those names were accepted as successful based on the basic fact that they could pay back the Troubled Asset Relief Funds borrowed from the US government.

Will see what comes up with the figures…

THE BIG ANNOUNCEMENT - II

Figures are drawing the actual picture of the US economy. Increase in unemployment in September is 263k. This is reversing the downward momentum between April and August with a slight increase from August figure. US cumulative unemployment is standing at 9.8% after September. Investors who are ready to get a swine flu from a sneeze in those days reacted quickly by bringing down FTSE 100 index at the first days of last quarter of the year.

Housing market is ringing the bells too. Reuters informs repossession of a house for every 13 seconds, bringing worries that 6million houses are likely to be repossessed for the next three years. Inevitable and painful lagging effects of unemployment...

Despite these facts; change in the moods between early-April and now is incredibly huge! A change from depression expectations to growth cheers! It is understandable when considering the catastrophic nature of the first quarter of 2009 where we saw falls of 45.7% in Japan's exports, 47% in German engineering companies' export orders. And only in one single month! Nobody wants to even imagine what would happen if this percentage falls continued.

Bernanke is now "carefully optimistic" with slight emphasis of the previous announcement by saying "Recession is very likely over" this time he has a "but", which is "It is still going to feel like a very weak economy for some time".

The announcement is turning from big into realistic. This is parallel to the fact that no rational person will believe in pink clouds, not after US households saw their wealth shrinking by $14trillion!

US economy expanded 3.5% in Q-3 2009 driven by consumption item.

Japan, inherited a huge debt burden from the previous crash of decade old with public debt of 180% of GDP. And recession lowered its tax revenue by $470billion.

Here is a short post from my blog:

JAPAN & DEFLATION

Japan's deflation problem since early 1990s have been ranked lower in priority during the recession following the globally imposed problems such as fall in exports, huge budget deficits caused by attempts to increase domestic demand through government spending, dealing with Debt to GDP ratio of over 180%.

Now deflation is back in an economy, which is trying to recover from recession. People don't spend as they expect the prices to fall more. With consumption item of GDP low, the burden is on investment and government spending. And without consumption, investment will be low too. Government issued ¥10,800billion ($110billion) bonds last fiscal year and announced a stimulus spending announcement of ¥7,200billion recently.

GROWTH MODELS: SUPPLY OR DEMAND DETERMINED

Now that the global world is growing again; one question that is coming to mind is: "Is it supply or demand determined?"
The answer is demand determined for the moment, meaning supply adjusts to demand. Economist Tinbergen's adjustment between demand and supply is in place, which is government regulating demand and supply to achieve the target/s of growth. All the recent government stimulus by developed economies are in mind.

Once the economy recovers and governments withdraw their support from the economy, the answer should change to supply determined, meaning price and market mechanism without state intervention.

5. MONETARY & FISCAL POLICY

Milton Friedman is the name coming to mind when talking about monetarism/monetary policy who is basically saying that money supply is the major determinant of short term demand in economy and therefore fiscal policy is rejected and also the government's role.

John Maynard Keynes is the name synchronized with fiscal policy.

During the current recession we had both expansionary monetary and fiscal policies combined with low interest rates.

US had the largest fiscal stimulus in history. Also broad money grew at an annualised rate of 1.2% for the six months between June 2009 and November 2009. Fed's supply of reserve funds increased from $942billion in September 2008 to $2.3trillion a year later.

Some government injections into the European economy since 2008 as of mid-January 2009 were: UK: $60billion, Netherlands: $42billion, Germany: $30billion, Belgium: $24billion.

In Asia; Japan's fiscal stimulus was 5trillion yen (US$51billion); China's was 4trillion yuan (US$584billion) in November 2008.

Then came the inevitable result of budget deficits. And the main challenge is to decide when to exit the expansion. Too early risks losing the confidence and having a double dip crash whereas too late risks getting wider budget deficits.

GLOBALISED EXIT

Following Jean-Claude Trichet's - President of European Central Bank - underlying the importance of large insurance companies and pension funds as important ingredients of systemic risk last month, a second announcement came out yesterday, which sounds like an indirect declaration of exit from expansionary monetary policy.

Federal Reserve has been cautiously testing the right time of the exit from quantitative easing since mid-October through reverse repos, which is basically pulling out the liquidity from the system through selling assets such as treasury bills. $1trillion additional liquidity was injected into the economy since the beginning of the crisis in 2007

2010 seems to be the year.

SHAPE OF RECESSION

There were many discussions on which letter of the alphabet the recession would end up with:

W: Double dip, two consecutive business cycles
V: Single dip
L: Economy going down and staying there for long.
I think, there is a need for a new letter to show that economy is balancing at lower level of income. "F" may be. We can think it in terms of Cartesian coordinates: x the horizontal axis, y the vertical axis and the top horizontal line (x1) of letter F as the level of income before recession and the below horizontal line (x2) as the level after the recession.

6. INTEREST RATES

Alan Greenspan in his article of "We need a better cushion against risk" is mentioning the fact that he had predicted the bubble to explode at several stages when he says:

"I feared "irrational exuberance" in 1996, but the dotcom bubble proceeded to inflate for another four years. Similarly, I opined in a federal open market committee meeting in 2002 that "it's hard to escape the conclusion that ... our extraordinary housing boom ... financed by very large increases in mortgage debt, cannot continue indefinitely into the future". The housing bubble did continue to inflate into 2006."

This is the reasoning behind the fact that Fed raised interest rates 17 consecutive times from 2003 until 2006 from 1% to 5.25%. In January 2001, the rate was 6%, which was a lowered level from 6.5%.

Bank of England cut the base rate from 2% to 1.5% in January 2009, which was the lowest level since the Bank was set up in 1694. In 1694 the reason was to provide finance for war whereas it was to fight against the recession this time.

7. BANKRUPTCIES

Portfolio of bankruptcies was diversified from auto, retail to banking. Some of the most established names which immediately come to mind are:

164 years old Lehman Brothers in September 2008, 100 years old Woolworths in December 2008, 250 years old Wedgwood in January 2009, 100 years old General Motors in June 2009, 85 years old Japanese Airlines in January 2010. General Motors was restructured as a new entity.

JAPANESE AIRLINES

One thing, which can only be seen as "the whole glass is empty" is bankruptcy. It can be quite nostalgic depending on how old the company is. Last year in UK the list of the big names included 100 years old Woolworths, 250 years old Wedgewood. The former being the choice of tight budget customers whereas the latter serving luxury looking customers. Both existed over many generations.

As we are going through 2010's first month, a new huge one came up from Japanese Airlines, which is Asia's biggest airline. This is the first bankruptcy of the industry at this scale during this recession. Japanese government's announcement of protection of creditors provided a relief. And it is a re-reminder of weak earnings considering the liquid nature of the business model.

The reason/s why this is so important will be the subject of my new blog post.

8. STOCK MARKETS

Stock market as a long term investment area is a proxy of wealth effect, which is an accumulated store of financial claims and possessions.

US stock market size was $22trillion as of first quarter of 2008, fell to $12trillion in October 2008 (one-third of $36trillion global size). The falls in October 2008 compared to a year go were 42% for Dow Jones, 46% for S&P 500 and 48% for Nasdaq. At the end of August 2009, S&P was at 1998 level. 2008 was declared as the worst year for
FTSE 100 index.

2nd of March 2009 was a recorded lowest level for many stock markets around the world. For FTSE 100 index, lowest level of the last six years with 18.9% fall during the first two months of the year; lowest level for S&P since November 1996 with losses of 21% accompanied with Dow Jones lowest level since 1997. MSCI World Index of 23 developed-country stock markets was already down by 22.9% for the year, which was the lowest level since it started at the end of 1969.

The shift in weights was also remarkable. In 2003 the stock markets of US, UK and Japan formed 73% of the value of the MSCI all-country index; by the end of 2009 this proportion was just 59%.

The market experienced budget cuts as well. In 2009 Alternative Investment Market (AIM) in UK, which is the stock market for small and medium sized businesses, saw companies choosing to delist in order to save £100thousand - £200thousand of annual costs.

9. MORTGAGE MARKETS

As another proxy of wealth effect, US housing market was creating significant wealth between 2001 and 2005 and had reached a size of $12trillion. But the value dropped to $7.1trillion as of the first quarter of 2008.

10. BOND MARKETS

When bank lending dried in debt-addicted economies, the ten-step ahead entrepreneurs needed to find a solution. Bond markets were one of them. They served the interests of governments and corporations so well that overall $1.5trillion was borrowed in the first quarter of 2009 of which $331billion of it was borrowed by companies. The overall figure in 2008 was $391billion.

On corporations' side; the companies, which were considered safest were able to borrow. Only in February, $136billion was raised globally and over half of it was raised by high credit rated companies. Roche alone raised $30billion to fund the takeover of Greentech – US biotech group. In order to attract investors, they paid premium over government bonds at record levels since 1930s.

Global bond issuance in 2009 was expected to hit $3trillion, a record in history with a split of $2trillion in US, $1trillion in Europe.

11. SPECULATIVE MOTIVE FOR HOLDING MONEY

Money is held for three main purposes:

Transactions
Store of value
Speculation
Speculative motive (future exchanges) hits the summit when the uncertainty about the future interest rates is highest. Money markets as proxy of speculative motive had $3,736billion at the end of 2008 in US's money market funds compared to $3,100billion at the end of 2007.

When the money supply is increased; money demand doesn't respond immediately/in the short-run. It takes a while until injection of money has its final effect on prices and trade can be boosted or depressed while prices adjust to changes in money supply.

12. PUBLIC DEBT & BUDGET DEFICIT

Governments worldwide in panic of filling the big hole left from the lack of consumption and investment spending had to step in the markets.

In 2009 the Euro zone governments agreed to raise €800bn, which was 23% up from 2008.

As the market for bonds was so crowded at the beginning of 2009, there weren't enough demand from investors for everyone. During the first quarter of 2009, Germany failed to raise the target €6billion through bonds sales, staying at the level of €5.24billion instead. Netherlands had the same experience with €2billion target. Spain and Belgium decided to cancel from the beginning due to lack of demand. UK and Italy could rise after offering higher yields to investors.

US was more confident in spending of $1trillion for the fiscal year starting from October 2008. The fact that US$ is a reserve currency is a main contributor to that.

UK's 2009/10 fiscal year plan of issuing £148billion of government bonds/gilts, which was slightly higher than 2008/09 and three fold of 2007/08, was adding to the nerves of investors of which 35% are foreign. The question was "Was that level of debt sustainable?"

13. PRIVATE DEBT

As an obligation of private individuals and corporations; private debt is to fund the consumption and investment elements of GDP, for the portion, which can not be funded out of incomes or revenues.
US private debt/GDP ratio was 123% in 1981; same figure was 290% in third quarter of 2008. Financial sector had the lion share with an increase from 22% of GDP to 117% during the same period.

14. REGULATION

We can take the origins of the concept to as far as 18th century's Britain when Parliamentary power's growth against the monarchy brought better stability of public finances, and more rational system of taxation.

Many regulations of United States have their origins in the responses given to Great Depression. More specifically, in 1933 federal government closed all US banks and permitted only those believed to be solvent to function.

Banking still remains to be one of the most regulated businesses today. However, most developed economies liberalized their financial systems and therefore loosened the regulations, especially in banking. Japan and Sweden in 1980s are few examples as discussed above.

15. FORECASTS NOT WORKING ANYMORE

One reality was non functioning forecasts, which kept changing on a regular basis mainly during the last quarter of 2008 and first quarter of 2009. This was one thing emphasized by CEOs attending World Economic Forum in Davos in 2009. "We can not predict anything" was a theme brought into attention.

IMF's global economic growth forecast for 2008 was 5% in 2007; updated to 3.7% in mid December 2008. US 2009 forecast growth updated from 2% to 0.1%

16. INVESTMENT

Investment is the most volatile component of GDP. Consumption and government spending are pretty much predictable; the former from propensity to consume and the latter from budgets planned in advance.

What makes investment so unpredictable? As Keynes mentioned, decisions to invest are driven by a mixture of "expectations, ignorance and uncertainty". These three form "animal spirits" approach to investment.

Current prices do not contain all the information to predict the future price. We are making investment decisions partly by hoping that the wind will back us, partly by taking risks depending on our risk attitudes. Whether we are averse, lover or neutral towards risk.

Also as put by Keynes when investment "runs ahead" of saving there has to be depression to enable savings to "catch up". We had 2008-2009 to catch up.

Speculative investment in the form of net capital flows to emerging markets fell from $1trillion to $160billion between 2007 and 2009.

Investment in infrastructure generates income above the expenditure. Because those expenditures will become income for others and those others will in turn spend most of what they receive. This makes this type of investment's effect big named as "investment multiplier". In the last quarter of 2008, manufacturing and non-manufacturing companies' business investment fell by 3.9%.

17. ASSET CLASSES

The four main asset classes are commodities, equities, bonds and hedge funds.
Together all these assets are the backbone of personal wealth industry, which is worth $11trillion and one-third of it is based in Switzerland.

Forbes found the global number of billionaires last year falling to 793 from 1125 and a report by Spectrem Group, a research company, saw a drop in the number of American millionaires from 9.2million to 6.7million between 2007 and 2008.

As the biggest consumer of the commodities market; China's demand was high for gold and oil. The country increased its gold reserves from 600 tonnes in 2003 to 1054 tonnes, which was recently valued at $1.95trillion.

Hedge funds were the asset class, which shrank significantly. $2 trillion worth hedge fund industry was expected to shrink to $1 trillion by the end of 2009, which was the Madoff's systemic risk imposing effect. 1471 (15%) hedge funds closed down during 2008. They had to eliminate their borrowing as well.

The fears that the financial system was bankrupt peaked from third week of January 2009 onwards. Investors were confused for a long time. US money market funds investments increased to $3.7trillion at the end of 2008 from $3.1trillion one year ago. US central bank bought $300billion of Treasury bonds to move investors into Treasury bonds, which was 7% of a market size of $4.4trillion by then. From the third week of March 2009 until the next six months, US equities purchase fell to something negligible from a level of $850billion in 2007.

Here are two posts on the most volatile commodity's prices.

OIL PRICES - I

The price of oil since it was first discovered in 1861 has always been one of the most volatile and carefully watched variables of the economy.

When OPEC raised the price by 70% in October 1973 and a further 130% in December 1973 and overall ten-fold between 1973 and 1980, it turned into a volatility creating source.

In 1980s, demand for oil and price declined due to efforts of oil importing countries to find alternative energies such as coal, natural gas and nuclear power and alternative sources such as Norway.

Then came production quotas of OPEC.

OIL PRICES – II

1990s was a low price period.
But prices started to increase again in 21st century pushed by higher demand.

Goldman Sachs as the biggest trader of energy derivatives had made a forecast in March 2005 that prices could jump as high as $105 per barrel from then present levels of $50.

In July 2008 we saw the price over $147.

Now it is below $70 again.
Where will it go from here?

The answer lies in the competition between substitution effect of alternative energies versus demand effect of existing energies. As there is only one world, alternative energies is what logic dictates.

In January 2009 oil prices fell as low as $38 per barrel caused by reduction in world consumption by 800thousand barrels per day.

18. BAILOUTS

High scale bailout was a crucial part due to organizations causing "systemic risk". The more interlinked the company to the rest of the economy the higher the risk.

In March 2009 FED chairman Ben Bernanke put it as: "Any firm whose failure would pose a systemic risk must receive especially close supervisory oversight of its risk-taking, risk management and financial condition, and be held to high capital and liquidity standards"

At macro level; $40billion IMF bailout money was spent as of mid December 2008 for countries including Hungary, Ukraine, Iceland, and Pakistan

19. TROUBLED ASSET RELIEF PROGRAMME (TARP)

Alan Greenspan recommended the $700bn TARP funds to be used in a variety of ways to support the economy, including loans to carmakers and direct investments in banks.

The planned split as of February 2009 was between purchasing banks' ordinary shares, AIG's preference shares, Citigroup and Bank of America' shares and loan guarantees, automakers' loans.

Tim Geithner, US Treasury secretary, said on 29th March 09 that US government had about $135bn left in its TARP.

20. PRIVATE EQUITY

Private equity has been an option of raising capital from institutional investors for unlisted companies.

Leveraged buyout and venture capital (VC) has been the most common types. Leveraged buyout involves acquiring the majority of a grown business significantly funded by debt whereas VC involves investing in a promising company at early stages.

Private equity capital invested in leveraged buyouts as of December 2008 were $450billion and they are struggling with the fact that banks are not providing loans for them anymore and investors are committing either less or no funds. In Europe, 2008 was the lowest buyouts seen for the last five years falling 61% from 2007 level of €185billion. UK private equity market fell 80%.

From October 2008 through March 2009, there were no VC backed IPO in US (first example of two consecutive quarters). As of mid February 2009; VC firms in UK – (there were 1100 VC backed companies by then) were warning the government that IPOs were not viable exit strategies and they needed to find an alternative way to exit from their investments.

21. BANKING

Nassim Nicholas Taleb, the author of "The Black Swan: The Impact of the Highly Improbable" said: "Save capitalism and free markets from the banks" in 2009 Davos World Economic Forum when he was expressing his anger to US TARP policy.

We need to bear in mind that today's financial world moved away from those days when banks were the dominant players. A significant share of the market includes big sectors such as insurance, foreign exchange, fund management, advisory services.

Banking industry works on a model where current ratio/short term liquidity is low. On the most rough/primitive sense loans sit on assets side and deposits on the liabilities. Usually loans are closer to being non-current assets as borrowers want to pay back over a time horizon such as 3-5-10-25 years whereas deposit holders on average want to have access to their money.

In crisis times, the situation gets worse. When confidence evaporates; individuals/businesses want to keep their liquidity under belt. The jump in relatively shorter term money market investments and run out on banks are in mind.

When crisis hit; all banks were fighting to get higher share of deposits. Concentration moved to capital, liquidity; lower reliance on short term borrowings and stable sources of funding such as deposits and longer-term debt. All these led to highly restricted lending of banks. They were focused on shrinking their balance sheets. Because the value of assets in balance sheets were falling due to falling loans and toxic sub prime securities.

Governments had to step into the economy. In mid October 2008, UK announced £37billion bailout for RBS, HBOS and Lloyds TSB. US allocated bailout funds of $700billion mainly for banks. Banks, which don't favour government intervention, looked for alternative ways of raising capital such as "Sovereign Wealth Funds".

Two banks, which made profits during those hard times, were Santander and Barclays.

Santander performed well, although it couldn't avoid being a victim of Madoff at a level of $2.87billion. When I had asked for the reason to a friend's partner who is one of its executive employees; he said "Santander's philosophy is to know the business it is doing very well." It has been very conscious on the importance of the capital strength with tier-1 capital of 6.31% in September 2008.

Similarly Barclays made a profit of £1.37billion in Q1-09, which was 15% higher compared to previous year. The lion portion was made by investment banking division with £1.05billion pre-tax profit and 189% increase from a year ago. The main factor was to take the opportunity of increasing market share with disappearance of big players from the market.

In February 2008, Financial Times had made a comparison between the investment banks, which recovered the crisis better and those, which couldn't. The better performers (JP Morgan Chase, Goldman Sachs, Deutsche Bank, Barclays Capital) were the ones, which had a strong reputation in the fixed-income business whereas the bad performers were the ones with strong reputation in equities business (UBS, Citigroup, Merrill Lynch, Morgan Stanley).

The sector wrote off assets of over $1trillion globally after a continuous growth of eight years from 1999 onwards. Is it over? Three expert sources' answers are:

a. IMF's Global Financial Stability Report:

The report at the end of third quarter in 2009 made a warning that Britain's banks have written only one-third of their losses on their balance sheets so far at the level of $110billion and predicted another $200billion of losses for the next two years. Same report emphasized that US banks written down half of losses, and European banks only 20%. The report calculated the new capital needs as $275billion for US banks, $375billion for Euro zone banks and $125billion for UK banks in order to achieve common equity/tangible assets ratio of 4%. This is a measure of financial strength, showing what ordinary shareholders will receive if the company is liquidated. IMF recommended governments to convert their shares in banks from preference shares to common equity.

Same report estimated global losses of $4.1trillion in loans. Industry wise banks making two-third and insurance companies, pension funds, hedge funds and others the rest.

b. Alan Greenspan's article titled "We need a better cushion against risk"

The article is a great resource to understand the challenges lying for US banking system. The key highlights for banking are mentioned as:

As of end of 2008; $500billion of $12trillion original book value US banks' commercial assets had been written off and another $500billion needed to be added. But the overall amount needed for going back to normal lending days would be $850billion. If equity prices turn up this burden would be lower.

c. FSA's Turner Review:

On 18th March 2009; Lord Turner, Chairman of FSA published the Turner Review, which identified three fundamental causes of the crisis as macroeconomic imbalances, "financial innovation of little social value", and deficiencies in key bank capital and liquidity regulations. The report emphasized that these three factors got their roots from "rational and self correcting markets" theory. As a solution to risk concerns; FSA asked the banks to have tier 1 capital reserves/assets ratio to be 6%-7%. The banks followed the capital requirement of the report as Barclays increased from 7.9% to 9.5%; HSBC from 8.8% to 8.9%; Lloyds TSB from 8.6% to 9%; RBS from 8.6% to 11.6% between 30 June 2008 and 21 January 2009.

In 1840s banks were holding capital at 50% of the book value of their assets.

Here are two related blog posts:

NEW COMPETITION TREND: REPAY TARP FUND

This week we saw an interesting request from Goldman Sachs to pay back the $10billion government bail out money received through Troubled Asset Relief Program (TARP). Follower JP Morgan Chase announced it has enough money to pay back $25billion bailout funds. Both announced good profit figures to strengthen their requests.
At a time when government is about to announce the results of stress tests for the top nineteen US banks and conclude whether there is need for further capital injections from $700bn TARP, it is a question mark whether Goldman Sachs & JP Morgan Chase's timing are good. What might be the motivation behind the new competition trend?

Top Wall Street banks seem to be concerned about being rescued by government funds and restricted in all activities taken including executives' bonuses, and preference shareholders' dividends. The possible motivations can be summarized as:

1) Saving the reputation;
2) Getting back the independence of bonus, dividend paying;

3) Attracting clients through the message of "look, I am still the best, paying back the bailout funds first"
4) Diverting public anger.

The stakeholders' reaction to the new trend is not clear yet:

Markets digested the news positively today as JP Morgan Chase's share price increased by 3.65 per cent; Goldman Sachs's followed it by 0.72 per cent increase.
Government is the most cautious side with focus on the stress test results and determined not to add further to damaged confidence.
Clients will be watching carefully after losing billions of dollars in investments.

Executives and preference shareholders will be the most eager side as pressures on bonuses and dividends will be released.
Ordinary shareholders might take it as an increase in risk and therefore increase cost of capital.

Will these efforts help lowering the new shock caused by Chapter 11 bankruptcy protection sought by General Growth today? The biggest real estate failure with $29.26billion of assets and $27.29billion of debt.

We will find out soon.

NEW COMPETITION TREND: REPAY TARP FUND – II

After Bank of America's attempt last week, Citigroup is demanding to repay bail-out money received through TARP funds as well, which are $45billion and $20billion respectively.

In April, when Goldman Sachs and JP Morgan Chase had requested to repay $10billion and $25billion respectively, US government was much more cautious before deciding whether to accept it or not. But now the government officials are discussing one step ahead: "how shall we use these funds: more government spending and job creation or closing the budget deficit?"
This time markets are more cautious with initial response of a decline in Citigroup's share price today.

22. MARKET CAPITALIZATION

Global market capitalization, which is market price of shares multiplied by the number of shares, of banking and insurance sectors have changed significantly between August 2007 and January 2009. The figure was $8.5trillion in August 2007, $7.3trillion in March 2008, $5.9trillion in September 2008, $3.6trillion in January 2009.

23. EXCHANGE RATES

UK debt is forcing historical lows in sterling against the dollar. $/£: 1.3857, also against Japanese yen: Y124.18 as of beginning of 2009.

THREE MAJOR WESTERN CURRENCIES - I

Last year this time, sterling-euro exchange rate (€/£) was almost 1. 1£ was equivalent of 1€. This was from a level of 1.36 in January 2008, 1.44 in November 2007. (Now it is 1.11)

Similarly; dollar-sterling exchange rate ($/£) this time last year was 1.48, 1.98 in January 2008, 2.08 in November 2007. (Now it is 1.62)

One theory that would explain the movement is the inflation differences between the countries/regions. For $/£ between January 2008 and last time this year, there should be higher inflation in UK economy compared to the US economy according to the theory.

THREE MAJOR WESTERN CURRENCIES - II

Sterling devalued both against the euro and the US dollars in 2008.

During the year, US inflation was 1% on average and UK inflation was 3.5% (Note). The inflation discrepancy is 3.4% whereas the change in exchange rate is 25%.

For the same period, average Euro zone inflation was 3.3% against the UK inflation of around 3.5%. The inflation discrepancy in this case is almost negligible at 0.2% whereas the change in the exchange rate is higher at 36%.

Although the theory is right in the sense that UK has higher inflation rate and therefore devaluation of its currency, it is not sufficient in explaining the significant differences in this case.

Note: Consumer price index is used for inflation.

EURO MOVE

In a team work exercise I have been about seven years ago; two small groups were asked to build a tower from paper and staples.

Both groups were given "a" amount of papers, plenty of staples, "b" amount of capital. If ran out of paper you could buy more by "c" amount of money. For breakeven the tower should have been at least "d" foot tall and any foot above the breakeven would add to existing capital. The team, which would add more with consideration of scarce resource of papers would be the winner.

In my team (T1); we decided to make cylinder shaped blocks by rolling the papers - attached with staples- to make a cube of 3*3 (each cylinder making one of 9), and put some papers between each layer of 3*3. To make the foundation stronger; use three papers for each roll of the first two layers and roll them as landscape shaped. Then from third layer onwards use two papers for each roll and roll them as portrait shaped.

T1's building was getting higher and higher, as if competing to Eiffel Tower. When finished, I said, "Be careful with moving, the building may fall down" and two of the observers of the team as a joke acted like they were going to run. It didn't fall and T1 had the highest capital.

The link to today: Just reading Financial Times of Saturday and once more seeing how suddenly global economy can shake with one walk, worse if run. Just look what happened to Euro. An economy making 3% of the zone's GDP shook the whole Euro zone, and the value of the currency, causing 5% fall in the exchange rate against the US$ in 2010 so far. The market for Euro is moving strongly. And it may be the time to watch the Euro Zone Tower.

24. OFFSHORE CENTRES:

One of the proposals on the G20 summit held on 2nd April 2009 was fastening on tax havens or offshore financial centres. Worldwide offshore assets' value is $6trillion. Some industry dominated ones are: Cayman Islands providing home to world's hedge funds and 12thousand US corporations are based here; Bermuda home to insurance, Jersey home to fund management; Monaco home to rich residents; Switzerland home to foreign assets (35% of bank balance sheets).

B. MICRO

25. MANAGERIAL FAILURE

At micro level; short-termism reflected by focus on profit and loss account rather than balance sheet; greedy expansion funded by debt have been systemic risk creating factors.

Here is a post from my blog:

CORPORATE SOCIAL RESPONSIBILITY

Milton Friedman's 1970 article in New York Times said: "Social responsibility of a business is to increase its profits" He was mentioning the sole social responsibility of business being to increase its profits through using its resources and staying within the rules of the game. What are the rules of the game?

Firms supply goods and services with the objective of maximising shareholders' wealth. And they will have the sort of risks associated to this objective, such as losing customer satisfaction and therefore revenue; threat of new entries, substitutes; cost structure etc. Planning is needed for short, medium and long term in order to control the risks. It is very disappointing for most of us to see very big companies hitting the wall, giving the impression they have been doing business without understanding their business environment and without forecasting the next three to six months. Three names coming immediately to my mind are:

AIG - Eighteenth largest company in the world with 116,000 employees - swallowed $170bn of the US bailout funds so far, bringing the benefits of its survival under question.
General Motors – Second largest automaker in the world with 266,000 employees - New CEO is talking about Chapter 11 bankruptcy by 1 June 2009.

RBS –With 141,000 employees and 700 branches in UK - acquired ABN AMRO with a consortium on 9th October 2007 at record price of €70billion and spread contagious subprime mortgage assets. It still can not recover, announcing 9,000 more job cuts on Tuesday, the 7th April.

Current economic environment is witnessing new ones such as Lloyds TSB's merger with HBOS. It doesn't appear to be a digestible transaction as Lloyds TSB has fallen from top four ranks in terms of market capitalization in 1999 to disappearing from top fifty in 2009. Share price has fallen from 860p in 1999 to 79.50p in 2009.

I agree on the importance of regulation to avoid such big, macro failures happening again but also doubt if you can really control every firm. Firms should be able to appoint the right senior management, who can lead their companies. At least the big names like AIG, General Motors, and RBS!

Can we move to a more ethical ground in terms of doing business?

26. RIGHTS ISSUES

Rights issue is basically when companies need to raise additional capital, they need to go to existing shareholders first because of their pre-emptive rights and those new shares are offered to existing shareholders at a discounted price.

As a solution to reconstruct their balance sheets many companies sought rights issues.
Some examples are as below:
Societe General issue in February 2008, raising €5.5billion at a level of €47.50 (39% discount to its closing value of €77.72).

Scandinavian Airlines (SAS) issue in February 2009 at SKr6billion ($825million)

Rio Tinto rights issue of $8billion in April 2009. Premier Foods, Segro and Wolseley are the other names, which applied rights issues at heavy discounts.
Companies needed to apply huge discounts for persuading shareholders to use their pre-emptive rights.

27. DEBT

When we talk about debt; Franco Modigliani & Merton Miller are the two names coming to mind. Their original proposition was saying that value of a company is independent of the way it is financed, in other words, the value of a company financed with debt is the same as the value of a company financed with equity. This was based on one of the three assumptions that there is no tax. BUT when tax is introduced to their models, then the value of the company is higher when it is financed via debt. Why? Because interest is a tax deductible expense, which means it is lowering the tax you pay.

UK's FTSE 350 companies excluding banks and financial services firms had a debt of £210billion as of 2009 and £29billion of it needed to be paid within 2009, £52billion by 2010, £48billion by 2011.

"Too much of debt brought more harm than good", some companies applied debt restructuring. Ford swapped $10.4billion of its debt for equity in December 2008. Wolseley restructured its loan for €1billion new lending.

28. DIVIDEND CUTS

Dividends are paid to preference shareholders. The companies in the early stages may prefer not to pay dividends but instead grow the business or to invest in projects, which increase the value of the company.

Dividend announcements act as a "signalling mechanism". When you cut the dividends, the outside world is highly likely to interpret it that your company is doing bad unless you justify this by a public announcement saying "we have got some very promising projects we need to invest in and they will increase our profits by x% in y amount of time"

First quarter in 2009 was the worst performance of S&P in terms of dividend payments since the records began in 1955. 367 of the listed companies cut dividends as a record high and only 83 raised dividends as a record low. The prediction as of beginning of January 2009 was that S&P 500 companies' dividends would fall by 22.6%, which was the worst since 1938.

During the second half of 2009, General Electric cut dividend for 31 cents to 10 cents per share, which saved then $9billion annually. This was the first time General Electric did it since 1938.

Lufthansa cut dividends to 70cents per share from €1.25.

Capital One Financial Corporation cut dividends by 87% in March 2009.

29. STARS

Some companies are worth to mention as their performance improved during crisis, achieving to be "negatively correlated" to severe market conditions.

Thomson Reuters: Profit in third quarter of 2008 jumped to $381million from $3million a year ago. The main driver has been announced to be the foreign exchange applications from Iceland, Japan's currencies to convert to US$ and £. And September's foreign exchange volume was announced to be $1trillion.

Apple announced record sales in Q4-08. Also in Q1-09 profits rose to $1.21billion compared to $1.05billion one year ago.

Verizon's – second largest US phone company – profits for Q4-08 increased $1.2billion from $1.1billion one year ago.

Ericsson's operating profit for Q4-08 was 9.2billion SEK ($1.1billion) excluding restructuring costs of 3billion SEK.

30. HISTORICAL STARS SURPRISING

Yes, the companies which made us surprised and can't help saying "No company is recession proof then":

Google revenues in Q1-09 fell below the preceding quarter for the first time in the company's history as the global recession brought an end to its unprecedented 11-year growth spurt.

Microsoft's revenues fell for the first time in its 34 years of history in Q1-09.

Deutsche Bank made its first annual loss of €4.8billion in five decades as of 2008.

Nokia's 90% fall in net profit for Q1-09 to €122m. After 15 years of hyper growth for handset-makers, the handsets sold by Nokia were 93.2m in the quarter to March 31, down 19% compared with last year, reported revenue was €9.3bn, down 27%.

WINNING STRATEGY: COST LEADERSHIP

Anyone who has somehow touched business studies will recall Michael Porter's name. Porter -Harvard professor specialising in Management and Economics - describes three generic strategies of firms to gain competitive advantage as: cost leadership, differentiation and market segmentation or focus.

Differentiation has been an innovative and respectable way of entering to and staying in any market of which doing the business in a different way, challenging the available methods, thinking outside the box have been the main characteristics. However credit crunch is making it hard for differentiation to breath and pushing firms in most industries to be cost leader to increase their market share or in most cases to survive.

Swiss chocolate maker Lindt & Sprungli's closure of 62.5 per cent of its 80 retail boutiques in US is the most recent example of this. Lindt has a self defined philosophy of premium quality chocolate with products or services of superior quality and value and a history, which goes back to 1879. Being established and good quality can not prevent customers from moving to cheaper brands.

Asda and Lidl's increase in UK market share by the end of 2008 due to cheap products are other examples of success of the strategy in retail sector.
The problem with cost leadership is the squeezing profit margins, thanks to price sensitive buyers, which is a barrier to new entrants. However it will work well when there are economies of scale, learning effect, low costs for factors of production, technological developments.

If you can achieve these conditions adding minimum or best no debt in balance sheet, then you are likely to be a winner.

JAPANESE MIRACLES

Japan has been one of the miracle countries. On a land of nearly 80% of mountains unsuitable for agriculture they still managed to be the ninth largest producer of rice in the world, the main ingredient of their famous sushi. On a land of island being exposed to tsunamis, earthquakes they managed to build the houses, which can survive the earthquake at magnitude of 8.

Rank of number two in the league of global GDP, forth largest exporter and 6th largest importer plus enormous growth between 1960 and 1980 made the country a role model for the rest of the world in their management concepts such as kaizen (continuous improvement), just-in-time (production upon demand).

After their lost decade of 1990s, and a global world shaken by credit crunch, they are challenged again with an economy of deflation keeping the consumption low, weak earnings keeping investment low, government debt already with over 180% of GDP.

However, Japan managed to bring the exports, the only variable left to play with; in their favour in December 2009 at a level of ¥5.41trillion ($59billion). The country's exports are growing again after 15 months of consecutive fall. Yes, they are very below their peaks considering the fact that it was ¥12.7trillion ($113billion) in November 2007. What matters though is to gain the momentum of growth again.

Can Japan be heading to a new miracle of achieving good growth of GDP despite the challenges of depressed consumption, investment items and a government spending, which is restricted with a cumulatively high debt level and credit rating constraints?
The answer can be “yes”.

Lightning Source UK Ltd.
Milton Keynes UK
18 October 2010

161508UK00001B/1/P

9 781845 494247